K9 TRAINING LOG

This Search and Rescue K9 training log belongs to

_____

K9 Vaccination Records

Date_____

Vaccination_____

Date_____

Vaccination_____

Date_____

Vaccination_____

Allergies_____

Current Certifications

Certification_____

Expiration Date_____

Certification_____

Expiration Date_____

Certification_____

Expiration Date_____

Certification_____

Expiration Date_____

Notes

K9 Training Log

Temp _____

Date _____ Time

K9 _____

Handler _____

Age of tracks _____

Length of tracks _____

Articles used/found _____

Found end article/person

General Conditions

◯ Dry   ◯ Muggy   ◯ Wet   ◯ Light rain

◯ Heavy Rain   ◯ Snow   ◯ Sunny   ◯ Cloudy

◯ Overcast   ◯ Med rain

Terrain

◯ Pavement/cement/hard surface

◯ Grass   ◯ Bushy/forest   ◯ Rural

◯ Residential   ◯ Urban   ◯ Commercial

Wind Direction _____

◯ Still   ◯ Light   ◯ Med   ◯ Strong

Lighting Conditions

◯ Dark   ◯ Dawn   ◯ Daylight   ◯ Dusk

Map of the Training Area

↑
N

Handlers Notes:

_____
_____
_____
_____
_____
_____
_____
_____

Total time spent training today   _____
Accumulative time in this log to date   _____

K9 Training Log

Temp _____

Date _____ Time

K9 _____

Handler _____

Age of tracks _____

Length of tracks _____

Articles used/found _____

Found end article/person

General Conditions

◯ Dry ◯ Muggy ◯ Wet ◯ Light rain

◯ Heavy Rain ◯ Snow ◯ Sunny ◯ Cloudy

◯ Overcast ◯ Med rain

Terrain

◯ Pavement/cement/hard surface

◯ Grass ◯ Bushy/forest ◯ Rural

◯ Residential ◯ Urban ◯ Commercial

Wind Direction _____

◯ Still ◯ Light ◯ Med ◯ Strong

Lighting Conditions

◯ Dark ◯ Dawn ◯ Daylight ◯ Dusk

Map of the Training Area

Handlers Notes:

_____

_____

_____

_____

_____

_____

_____

_____

Total time spent training today   _____

Accumulative time in this log to date   _____

K9 Training Log

Temp _____

Date _____ Time

K9 _____

Handler _____

Age of tracks _____

Length of tracks _____

Articles used/found _____

Found end article/person

General Conditions

◯ Dry   ◯ Muggy   ◯ Wet   ◯ Light rain

◯ Heavy Rain   ◯ Snow   ◯ Sunny   ◯ Cloudy

◯ Overcast   ◯ Med rain

Terrain

◯ Pavement/cement/hard surface

◯ Grass   ◯ Bushy/forest   ◯ Rural

◯ Residential   ◯ Urban   ◯ Commercial

Wind Direction _____

◯ Still   ◯ Light   ◯ Med   ◯ Strong

Lighting Conditions

◯ Dark   ◯ Dawn   ◯ Daylight   ◯ Dusk

Map of the Training Area

Handlers Notes:

_____

_____

_____

_____

_____

_____

_____

_____

Total time spent training today   _____

Accumulative time in this log to date   _____

K9 Training Log

Temp _____

Date _____ Time

K9

Handler

Age of tracks

Length of tracks

Articles used/found

Found end article/person

General Conditions
◯ Dry ◯ Muggy ◯ Wet ◯ Light rain
◯ Heavy Rain ◯ Snow ◯ Sunny ◯ Cloudy
◯ Overcast ◯ Med rain

Terrain
◯ Pavement/cement/hard surface
◯ Grass ◯ Bushy/forest ◯ Rural
◯ Residential ◯ Urban ◯ Commercial

Wind Direction _____
◯ Still ◯ Light ◯ Med ◯ Strong

Lighting Conditions
◯ Dark ◯ Dawn ◯ Daylight ◯ Dusk

Map of the Training Area

Handlers Notes:

_____

_____

_____

_____

_____

_____

_____

_____

Total time spent training today   _____

Accumulative time in this log to date   _____

K9 Training Log

Temp _____

Date _____ Time _____

K9 _____

Handler _____

Age of tracks _____

Length of tracks _____

Articles used/found _____

Found end article/person

General Conditions
◯ Dry ◯ Muggy ◯ Wet ◯ Light rain
◯ Heavy Rain ◯ Snow ◯ Sunny ◯ Cloudy
◯ Overcast ◯ Med rain

Terrain
◯ Pavement/cement/hard surface
◯ Grass ◯ Bushy/forest ◯ Rural
◯ Residential ◯ Urban ◯ Commercial

Wind Direction _____
◯ Still ◯ Light ◯ Med ◯ Strong

Lighting Conditions
◯ Dark ◯ Dawn ◯ Daylight ◯ Dusk

Map of the Training Area

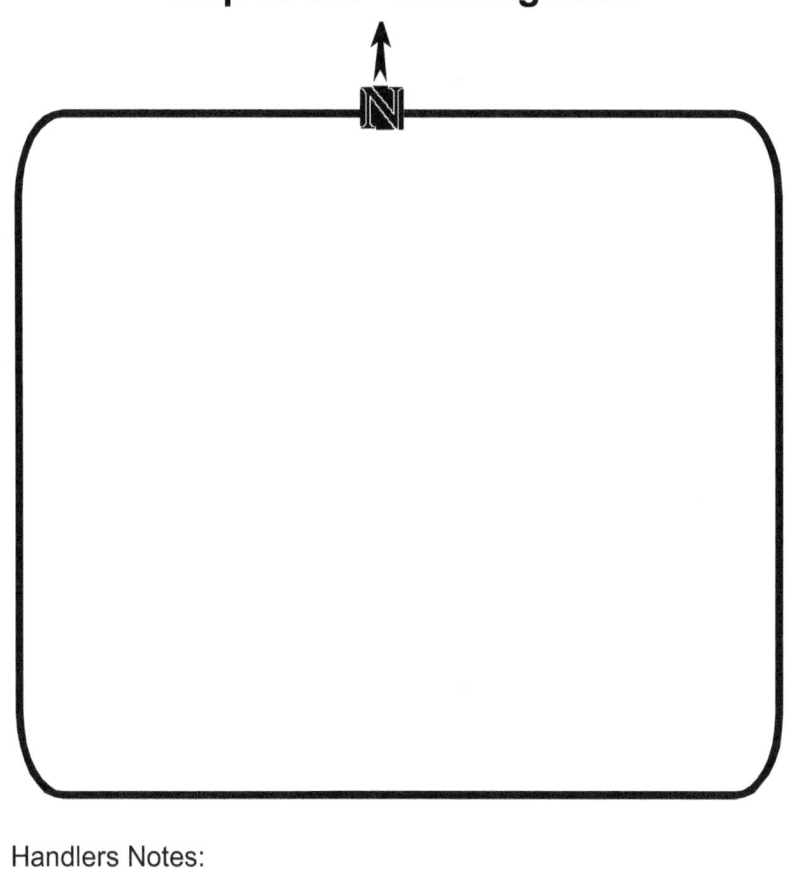

Handlers Notes:

_____

_____

_____

_____

_____

_____

_____

_____

Total time spent training today   _____
Accumulative time in this log to date   _____

K9 Training Log

Temp _____

Date _____ Time _____

K9 _____

Handler _____

Age of tracks _____

Length of tracks _____

Articles used/found _____

Found end article/person

General Conditions

◯ Dry ◯ Muggy ◯ Wet ◯ Light rain

◯ Heavy Rain ◯ Snow ◯ Sunny ◯ Cloudy

◯ Overcast ◯ Med rain

Terrain

◯ Pavement/cement/hard surface

◯ Grass ◯ Bushy/forest ◯ Rural

◯ Residential ◯ Urban ◯ Commercial

Wind Direction _____

◯ Still ◯ Light ◯ Med ◯ Strong

Lighting Conditions

◯ Dark ◯ Dawn ◯ Daylight ◯ Dusk

Map of the Training Area

Handlers Notes:

_____

_____

_____

_____

_____

_____

_____

_____

Total time spent training today   _____

Accumulative time in this log to date   _____

K9 Training Log

Temp _____

Date _____ Time _____

K9 _____

Handler _____

Age of tracks _____

Length of tracks _____

Articles used/found _____

Found end article/person

General Conditions

◯ Dry ◯ Muggy ◯ Wet ◯ Light rain
◯ Heavy Rain ◯ Snow ◯ Sunny ◯ Cloudy
◯ Overcast ◯ Med rain

Terrain

◯ Pavement/cement/hard surface
◯ Grass ◯ Bushy/forest ◯ Rural
◯ Residential ◯ Urban ◯ Commercial

Wind Direction _____

◯ Still ◯ Light ◯ Med ◯ Strong

Lighting Conditions

◯ Dark ◯ Dawn ◯ Daylight ◯ Dusk

Map of the Training Area

N

Handlers Notes:

_____

_____

_____

_____

_____

_____

_____

_____

Total time spent training today   _____

Accumulative time in this log to date   _____

K9 Training Log

Temp _____

Date _____ Time

K9

Handler

Age of tracks

Length of tracks

Articles used/found

Found end article/person

General Conditions

◯ Dry ◯ Muggy ◯ Wet ◯ Light rain

◯ Heavy Rain ◯ Snow ◯ Sunny ◯ Cloudy

◯ Overcast ◯ Med rain

Terrain

◯ Pavement/cement/hard surface

◯ Grass ◯ Bushy/forest ◯ Rural

◯ Residential ◯ Urban ◯ Commercial

Wind Direction _____

◯ Still ◯ Light ◯ Med ◯ Strong

Lighting Conditions

◯ Dark ◯ Dawn ◯ Daylight ◯ Dusk

Map of the Training Area

N

Handlers Notes:

_____

_____

_____

_____

_____

_____

_____

_____

Total time spent training today   _____

Accumulative time in this log to date   _____

K9 Training Log

Temp _____

Date _____ Time _____

K9 _____

Handler _____

Age of tracks _____

Length of tracks _____

Articles used/found _____

Found end article/person

General Conditions

◯ Dry ◯ Muggy ◯ Wet ◯ Light rain

◯ Heavy Rain ◯ Snow ◯ Sunny ◯ Cloudy

◯ Overcast ◯ Med rain

Terrain

◯ Pavement/cement/hard surface

◯ Grass ◯ Bushy/forest ◯ Rural

◯ Residential ◯ Urban ◯ Commercial

Wind Direction _____

◯ Still ◯ Light ◯ Med ◯ Strong

Lighting Conditions

◯ Dark ◯ Dawn ◯ Daylight ◯ Dusk

Map of the Training Area

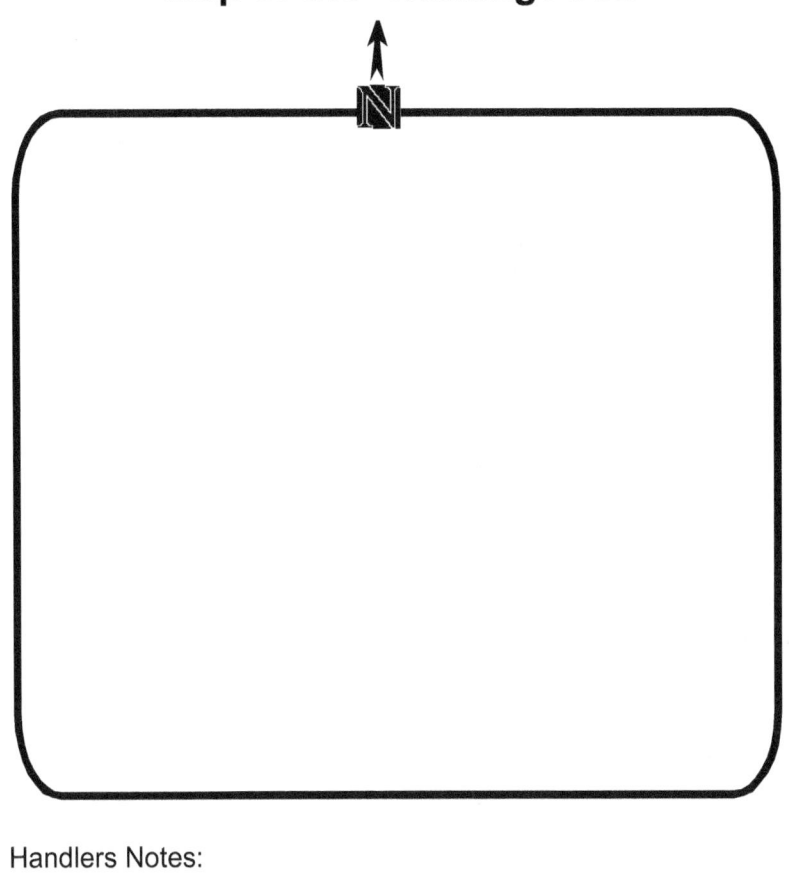

Handlers Notes:

_____

_____

_____

_____

_____

_____

_____

_____

Total time spent training today   _____

Accumulative time in this log to date   _____

K9 Training Log

Temp _____

Date _____ Time

K9

Handler

Age of tracks

Length of tracks

Articles used/found

Found end article/person

General Conditions

◯ Dry ◯ Muggy ◯ Wet ◯ Light rain

◯ Heavy Rain ◯ Snow ◯ Sunny ◯ Cloudy

◯ Overcast ◯ Med rain

Terrain

◯ Pavement/cement/hard surface

◯ Grass ◯ Bushy/forest ◯ Rural

◯ Residential ◯ Urban ◯ Commercial

Wind Direction _____

◯ Still ◯ Light ◯ Med ◯ Strong

Lighting Conditions

◯ Dark ◯ Dawn ◯ Daylight ◯ Dusk

Map of the Training Area

Handlers Notes:

_____

_____

_____

_____

_____

_____

_____

_____

Total time spent training today   _____

Accumulative time in this log to date   _____

K9 Training Log

Temp _____

Date _____ Time _____

K9 _____

Handler _____

Age of tracks _____

Length of tracks _____

Articles used/found _____

Found end article/person

General Conditions

◯ Dry ◯ Muggy ◯ Wet ◯ Light rain

◯ Heavy Rain ◯ Snow ◯ Sunny ◯ Cloudy

◯ Overcast ◯ Med rain

Terrain

◯ Pavement/cement/hard surface

◯ Grass ◯ Bushy/forest ◯ Rural

◯ Residential ◯ Urban ◯ Commercial

Wind Direction _____

◯ Still ◯ Light ◯ Med ◯ Strong

Lighting Conditions

◯ Dark ◯ Dawn ◯ Daylight ◯ Dusk

Map of the Training Area

N

Handlers Notes:

_____

_____

_____

_____

_____

_____

_____

_____

Total time spent training today   _____

Accumulative time in this log to date   _____

K9 Training Log

Temp _____

Date _____ Time _____

K9 _____

Handler _____

Age of tracks _____

Length of tracks _____

Articles used/found _____

Found end article/person

General Conditions

◯ Dry   ◯ Muggy   ◯ Wet   ◯ Light rain
◯ Heavy Rain   ◯ Snow   ◯ Sunny   ◯ Cloudy
◯ Overcast   ◯ Med rain

Terrain

◯ Pavement/cement/hard surface
◯ Grass   ◯ Bushy/forest   ◯ Rural
◯ Residential   ◯ Urban   ◯ Commercial

Wind Direction _____

◯ Still   ◯ Light   ◯ Med   ◯ Strong

Lighting Conditions

◯ Dark   ◯ Dawn   ◯ Daylight   ◯ Dusk

Map of the Training Area

↑
N

Handlers Notes:

_____

_____

_____

_____

_____

_____

_____

_____

Total time spent training today   _____

Accumulative time in this log to date   _____

K9 Training Log

Temp _____

Date _____ Time _____

K9 _____

Handler _____

Age of tracks _____

Length of tracks _____

Articles used/found _____

Found end article/person

General Conditions
◯ Dry ◯ Muggy ◯ Wet ◯ Light rain
◯ Heavy Rain ◯ Snow ◯ Sunny ◯ Cloudy
◯ Overcast ◯ Med rain

Terrain
◯ Pavement/cement/hard surface
◯ Grass ◯ Bushy/forest ◯ Rural
◯ Residential ◯ Urban ◯ Commercial

Wind Direction _____
◯ Still ◯ Light ◯ Med ◯ Strong

Lighting Conditions
◯ Dark ◯ Dawn ◯ Daylight ◯ Dusk

Map of the Training Area

↑
N

Handlers Notes:

_____

_____

_____

_____

_____

_____

_____

_____

Total time spent training today   _____
Accumulative time in this log to date   _____

K9 Training Log

Temp _____

Date _____ Time

K9

Handler

Age of tracks

Length of tracks

Articles used/found

Found end article/person

General Conditions

◯ Dry ◯ Muggy ◯ Wet ◯ Light rain

◯ Heavy Rain ◯ Snow ◯ Sunny ◯ Cloudy

◯ Overcast ◯ Med rain

Terrain

◯ Pavement/cement/hard surface

◯ Grass ◯ Bushy/forest ◯ Rural

◯ Residential ◯ Urban ◯ Commercial

Wind Direction _____

◯ Still ◯ Light ◯ Med ◯ Strong

Lighting Conditions

◯ Dark ◯ Dawn ◯ Daylight ◯ Dusk

Map of the Training Area

N

Handlers Notes:

_____

_____

_____

_____

_____

_____

_____

_____

Total time spent training today   _____

Accumulative time in this log to date   _____

K9 Training Log

Temp _____

Date _____ Time

_____
K9

_____
Handler

_____
Age of tracks

_____
Length of tracks

_____
Articles used/found

_____
Found end article/person

General Conditions

◯ Dry ◯ Muggy ◯ Wet ◯ Light rain
◯ Heavy Rain ◯ Snow ◯ Sunny ◯ Cloudy
◯ Overcast ◯ Med rain

Terrain

◯ Pavement/cement/hard surface
◯ Grass ◯ Bushy/forest ◯ Rural
◯ Residential ◯ Urban ◯ Commercial

Wind Direction _____

◯ Still ◯ Light ◯ Med ◯ Strong

Lighting Conditions

◯ Dark ◯ Dawn ◯ Daylight ◯ Dusk

Map of the Training Area

N

Handlers Notes:

_____

_____

_____

_____

_____

_____

_____

_____

Total time spent training today   _____

Accumulative time in this log to date   _____

K9 Training Log

Temp _____

Date _____ Time

K9 _____

Handler _____

Age of tracks _____

Length of tracks _____

Articles used/found _____

Found end article/person

General Conditions

◯ Dry ◯ Muggy ◯ Wet ◯ Light rain

◯ Heavy Rain ◯ Snow ◯ Sunny ◯ Cloudy

◯ Overcast ◯ Med rain

Terrain

◯ Pavement/cement/hard surface

◯ Grass ◯ Bushy/forest ◯ Rural

◯ Residential ◯ Urban ◯ Commercial

Wind Direction _____

◯ Still ◯ Light ◯ Med ◯ Strong

Lighting Conditions

◯ Dark ◯ Dawn ◯ Daylight ◯ Dusk

Map of the Training Area

↑
N

Handlers Notes:

_____

_____

_____

_____

_____

_____

_____

_____

Total time spent training today   _____

Accumulative time in this log to date   _____

K9 Training Log

Temp _____

Date _____ Time _____

K9 _____

Handler _____

Age of tracks _____

Length of tracks _____

Articles used/found _____

Found end article/person _____

General Conditions

◯ Dry ◯ Muggy ◯ Wet ◯ Light rain

◯ Heavy Rain ◯ Snow ◯ Sunny ◯ Cloudy

◯ Overcast ◯ Med rain

Terrain

◯ Pavement/cement/hard surface

◯ Grass ◯ Bushy/forest ◯ Rural

◯ Residential ◯ Urban ◯ Commercial

Wind Direction _____

◯ Still ◯ Light ◯ Med ◯ Strong

Lighting Conditions

◯ Dark ◯ Dawn ◯ Daylight ◯ Dusk

Map of the Training Area

N

Handlers Notes:

_____

_____

_____

_____

_____

_____

_____

_____

Total time spent training today   _____

Accumulative time in this log to date   _____

K9 Training Log

Temp _____

Date _____ Time _____

K9 _____

Handler _____

Age of tracks _____

Length of tracks _____

Articles used/found _____

Found end article/person _____

General Conditions
- ◯ Dry ◯ Muggy ◯ Wet ◯ Light rain
- ◯ Heavy Rain ◯ Snow ◯ Sunny ◯ Cloudy
- ◯ Overcast ◯ Med rain

Terrain
- ◯ Pavement/cement/hard surface
- ◯ Grass ◯ Bushy/forest ◯ Rural
- ◯ Residential ◯ Urban ◯ Commercial

Wind Direction _____
- ◯ Still ◯ Light ◯ Med ◯ Strong

Lighting Conditions
- ◯ Dark ◯ Dawn ◯ Daylight ◯ Dusk

Map of the Training Area

↑
N

Handlers Notes:

_____

_____

_____

_____

_____

_____

_____

_____

Total time spent training today   _____

Accumulative time in this log to date   _____

K9 Training Log

Temp _____

Date _____ Time

K9 _____

Handler _____

Age of tracks _____

Length of tracks _____

Articles used/found _____

Found end article/person _____

General Conditions

◯ Dry ◯ Muggy ◯ Wet ◯ Light rain

◯ Heavy Rain ◯ Snow ◯ Sunny ◯ Cloudy

◯ Overcast ◯ Med rain

Terrain

◯ Pavement/cement/hard surface

◯ Grass ◯ Bushy/forest ◯ Rural

◯ Residential ◯ Urban ◯ Commercial

Wind Direction _____

◯ Still ◯ Light ◯ Med ◯ Strong

Lighting Conditions

◯ Dark ◯ Dawn ◯ Daylight ◯ Dusk

Map of the Training Area

↑
N

Handlers Notes:

_____

_____

_____

_____

_____

_____

_____

_____

Total time spent training today   _____

Accumulative time in this log to date   _____

K9 Training Log

Temp _____

Date _____ Time _____

K9 _____

Handler _____

Age of tracks _____

Length of tracks _____

Articles used/found _____

Found end article/person

General Conditions

◯ Dry ◯ Muggy ◯ Wet ◯ Light rain

◯ Heavy Rain ◯ Snow ◯ Sunny ◯ Cloudy

◯ Overcast ◯ Med rain

Terrain

◯ Pavement/cement/hard surface

◯ Grass ◯ Bushy/forest ◯ Rural

◯ Residential ◯ Urban ◯ Commercial

Wind Direction _____

◯ Still ◯ Light ◯ Med ◯ Strong

Lighting Conditions

◯ Dark ◯ Dawn ◯ Daylight ◯ Dusk

Map of the Training Area

Handlers Notes:

_____

_____

_____

_____

_____

_____

_____

_____

Total time spent training today   _____
Accumulative time in this log to date   _____

K9 Training Log

Temp _____

Date _____ Time _____

K9 _____

Handler _____

Age of tracks _____

Length of tracks _____

Articles used/found _____

Found end article/person

General Conditions

◯ Dry ◯ Muggy ◯ Wet ◯ Light rain

◯ Heavy Rain ◯ Snow ◯ Sunny ◯ Cloudy

◯ Overcast ◯ Med rain

Terrain

◯ Pavement/cement/hard surface

◯ Grass ◯ Bushy/forest ◯ Rural

◯ Residential ◯ Urban ◯ Commercial

Wind Direction _____

◯ Still ◯ Light ◯ Med ◯ Strong

Lighting Conditions

◯ Dark ◯ Dawn ◯ Daylight ◯ Dusk

Map of the Training Area

Handlers Notes:

_____

_____

_____

_____

_____

_____

_____

_____

_____

Total time spent training today   _____
Accumulative time in this log to date   _____

K9 Training Log

Temp _____

Date _____ Time _____

K9 _____

Handler _____

Age of tracks _____

Length of tracks _____

Articles used/found _____

Found end article/person _____

General Conditions

◯ Dry ◯ Muggy ◯ Wet ◯ Light rain

◯ Heavy Rain ◯ Snow ◯ Sunny ◯ Cloudy

◯ Overcast ◯ Med rain

Terrain

◯ Pavement/cement/hard surface

◯ Grass ◯ Bushy/forest ◯ Rural

◯ Residential ◯ Urban ◯ Commercial

Wind Direction _____

◯ Still ◯ Light ◯ Med ◯ Strong

Lighting Conditions

◯ Dark ◯ Dawn ◯ Daylight ◯ Dusk

Map of the Training Area

↑
N

Handlers Notes:

_____

_____

_____

_____

_____

_____

_____

Total time spent training today _____

Accumulative time in this log to date _____

K9 Training Log

Temp _____

Date _____ Time _____

K9 _____

Handler _____

Age of tracks _____

Length of tracks _____

Articles used/found _____

Found end article/person _____

General Conditions

◯ Dry   ◯ Muggy   ◯ Wet   ◯ Light rain

◯ Heavy Rain   ◯ Snow   ◯ Sunny   ◯ Cloudy

◯ Overcast   ◯ Med rain

Terrain

◯ Pavement/cement/hard surface

◯ Grass   ◯ Bushy/forest   ◯ Rural

◯ Residential   ◯ Urban   ◯ Commercial

Wind Direction _____

◯ Still   ◯ Light   ◯ Med   ◯ Strong

Lighting Conditions

◯ Dark   ◯ Dawn   ◯ Daylight   ◯ Dusk

Map of the Training Area

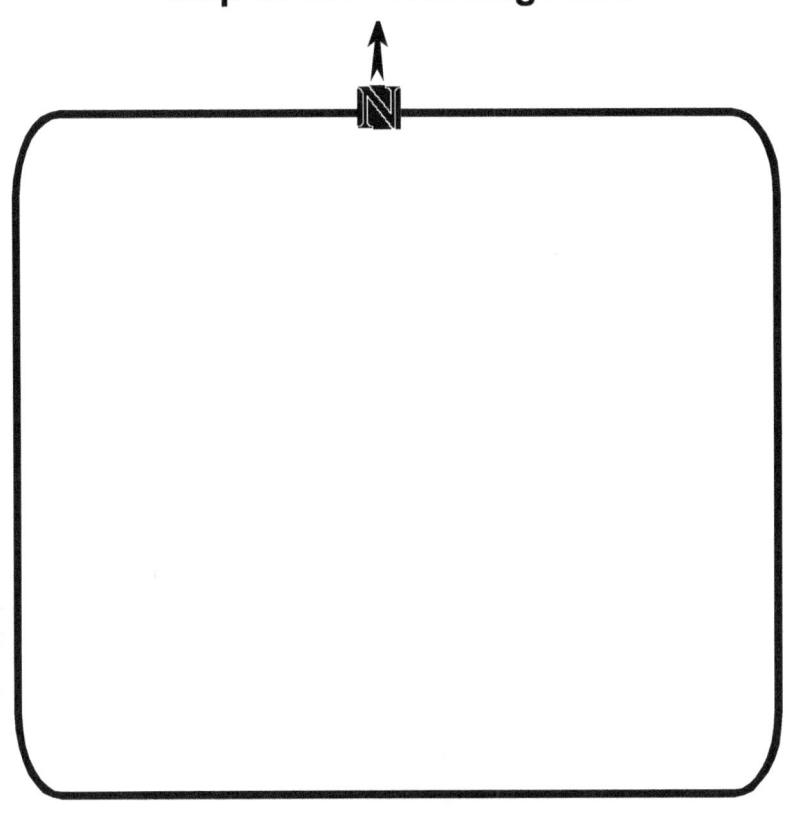

Handlers Notes:

_____

_____

_____

_____

_____

_____

_____

_____

Total time spent training today   _____
Accumulative time in this log to date   _____

K9 Training Log

Temp _____

Date _____ Time _____

K9 _____

Handler _____

Age of tracks _____

Length of tracks _____

Articles used/found _____

Found end article/person _____

General Conditions

◯ Dry ◯ Muggy ◯ Wet ◯ Light rain
◯ Heavy Rain ◯ Snow ◯ Sunny ◯ Cloudy
◯ Overcast ◯ Med rain

Terrain

◯ Pavement/cement/hard surface
◯ Grass ◯ Bushy/forest ◯ Rural
◯ Residential ◯ Urban ◯ Commercial

Wind Direction _____

◯ Still ◯ Light ◯ Med ◯ Strong

Lighting Conditions

◯ Dark ◯ Dawn ◯ Daylight ◯ Dusk

Map of the Training Area

Handlers Notes:

_____

_____

_____

_____

_____

_____

_____

_____

Total time spent training today   _____
Accumulative time in this log to date   _____

K9 Training Log

Temp _____

Date _____ Time

K9 _____

Handler _____

Age of tracks _____

Length of tracks _____

Articles used/found _____

Found end article/person

General Conditions

◯ Dry   ◯ Muggy   ◯ Wet   ◯ Light rain

◯ Heavy Rain   ◯ Snow   ◯ Sunny   ◯ Cloudy

◯ Overcast   ◯ Med rain

Terrain

◯ Pavement/cement/hard surface

◯ Grass   ◯ Bushy/forest   ◯ Rural

◯ Residential   ◯ Urban   ◯ Commercial

Wind Direction _____

◯ Still   ◯ Light   ◯ Med   ◯ Strong

Lighting Conditions

◯ Dark   ◯ Dawn   ◯ Daylight   ◯ Dusk

Map of the Training Area

N

Handlers Notes:

_____

_____

_____

_____

_____

_____

_____

Total time spent training today   _____

Accumulative time in this log to date   _____

K9 Training Log

Temp _____

Date _____ Time _____

K9 _____

Handler _____

Age of tracks _____

Length of tracks _____

Articles used/found _____

Found end article/person

General Conditions
◯ Dry   ◯ Muggy   ◯ Wet   ◯ Light rain

◯ Heavy Rain   ◯ Snow   ◯ Sunny   ◯ Cloudy

◯ Overcast   ◯ Med rain

Terrain
◯ Pavement/cement/hard surface

◯ Grass   ◯ Bushy/forest   ◯ Rural

◯ Residential   ◯ Urban   ◯ Commercial

Wind Direction _____
◯ Still   ◯ Light   ◯ Med   ◯ Strong

Lighting Conditions
◯ Dark   ◯ Dawn   ◯ Daylight   ◯ Dusk

Map of the Training Area

N

Handlers Notes:

_____

_____

_____

_____

_____

_____

_____

_____

Total time spent training today   _____
Accumulative time in this log to date   _____

K9 Training Log

Temp _____

Date _____ Time _____

K9 _____

Handler _____

Age of tracks _____

Length of tracks _____

Articles used/found _____

Found end article/person

General Conditions
◯ Dry ◯ Muggy ◯ Wet ◯ Light rain
◯ Heavy Rain ◯ Snow ◯ Sunny ◯ Cloudy
◯ Overcast ◯ Med rain

Terrain
◯ Pavement/cement/hard surface
◯ Grass ◯ Bushy/forest ◯ Rural
◯ Residential ◯ Urban ◯ Commercial

Wind Direction _____
◯ Still ◯ Light ◯ Med ◯ Strong

Lighting Conditions
◯ Dark ◯ Dawn ◯ Daylight ◯ Dusk

Map of the Training Area

↑
N

Handlers Notes:

_____

_____

_____

_____

_____

_____

_____

_____

Total time spent training today   _____

Accumulative time in this log to date   _____

K9 Training Log

Temp _____

Date _____ Time _____

K9 _____

Handler _____

Age of tracks _____

Length of tracks _____

Articles used/found _____

Found end article/person _____

General Conditions

◯ Dry ◯ Muggy ◯ Wet ◯ Light rain

◯ Heavy Rain ◯ Snow ◯ Sunny ◯ Cloudy

◯ Overcast ◯ Med rain

Terrain

◯ Pavement/cement/hard surface

◯ Grass ◯ Bushy/forest ◯ Rural

◯ Residential ◯ Urban ◯ Commercial

Wind Direction _____

◯ Still ◯ Light ◯ Med ◯ Strong

Lighting Conditions

◯ Dark ◯ Dawn ◯ Daylight ◯ Dusk

Map of the Training Area

↑
N

Handlers Notes:

_____

_____

_____

_____

_____

_____

_____

Total time spent training today   _____

Accumulative time in this log to date   _____

Notes

Notes

Notes